TRAPPED

Glenn Cheney

SADDLEBACK
EDUCATIONAL PUBLISHING

ASTONISHING HEADLINES

Attacked

Captured

Condemned

Kidnapped

Lost and Found

Missing

Shot Down

Stowed Away

Stranded at Sea

Trapped

SADDLEBACK
EDUCATIONAL PUBLISHING
www.sdlback.com

Copyright © 2005, 2013 by Saddleback Educational Publishing
All rights reserved. No part of this book may be reproduced in any form or by any means, electronic or mechanical, including photocopying, recording, scanning, or by any information storage and retrieval system, without the written permission of the publisher. SADDLEBACK EDUCATIONAL PUBLISHING and any associated logos are trademarks and/or registered trademarks of Saddleback Educational Publishing.

ISBN-13: 978-1-61651-927-8
ISBN-10: 1-61651-927-4
eBook: 978-1-61247-084-9

Printed in Guangzhou, China
NOR/0514/CA21400718

18 17 16 15 14   2 3 4 5 6

Photo Credits: Cover, Reuters Photo Archive; page 13, Picture History; page 39, Fedoseyev Lev, Itar-Tass Photos; pages 66–67, Matt Sullivan / Getty Images News / Getty Images; page 74, Alexey Stiop | Dreamstime.com; page 77, Ivan Cholakov | Dreamstime.com; page 87, AFP / AFP / Getty Images

CONTENTS

INTRODUCTION

What could be more terrifying than being trapped? You think there is no escape. There may be no time for rescue. Your whole life is replayed in your mind. You are trapped, and it looks as if there is no way out. Stay calm. Do not lose control. Use your wits. Maybe help is on the way.

Think of all the ways that people can be trapped. A fire can trap them in a building. The sea can trap them in a submarine. A flood can trap them on high ground. After an earthquake, people may be trapped under building rubble. Sometimes, governments trap their people behind walls, both real and imagined.

Watch Out for Traps

What is the best way to stay out of a trap? Think ahead. See the trap before it traps you.

- In a movie theater, plane, or hotel, look for the emergency exits.
- On a ship, look for lifeboats and life preservers.
- In a car or school bus, know how to unlock the door or use the emergency exit.
- At home, think of all the ways you can get out if there is a fire.
- Do not put a hand or foot into a big machine or farm equipment.

If someone else is trapped, dial 9-1-1 on any telephone. If you are trapped, do not panic—think. Let your brain be your friend, not your enemy.

The Triangle Shirtwaist Fire
DATAFILE

Timeline

May 1908

The first skyscraper, the Singer Building, is built in New York City.

March 1911

A fire at the Triangle Shirtwaist factory in New York kills 146.

Where is New York City?

HERE

Key Terms

fire escape—stairs outside a building that give people a way to escape a fire

inspector—a person who is hired to check for problems

sweatshop—a hot, crowded, unsafe shop or factory in which employees work long hours at low wages

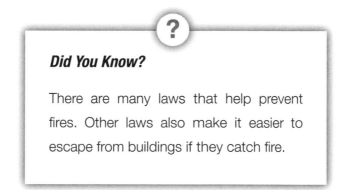

Did You Know?

There are many laws that help prevent fires. Other laws also make it easier to escape from buildings if they catch fire.

The Triangle Shirtwaist Fire

On March 25, 1911, a deadly fire in a New York factory killed 146 people.

The Triangle Shirtwaist Company made shirts. A shirtwaist was a blouse for women. The fabric was light and silky. But it burned easily.

The Triangle Shirtwaist factory was a 10-story building in New York City. Hundreds of people worked there. They cut cloth, sewed shirts, and packed boxes.

Sweatshops

It was not a nice place to work. The pay was very low. The work was hard. The rooms were hot and crowded. Employees worked seven days a week.

Almost all of the workers were women and children. The company hired children because they worked for less money. Some children were only 11 years old. Factories like these are called sweat-shops.

Worst of all, the bosses kept most of the windows and the doors locked. The workers could not go outside until it was time to quit. They were locked in!

Children Hid

The law said that children could not work in a factory. Sometimes inspectors came to look for children. The children hid under piles of shirts. No one saw them.

No one liked working in the factory. But in those days, it was hard to find a job. Without a job, people could not buy food or pay rent. When a worker found a job, he or she stayed with it.

Fire!

The fire started on the eighth floor of the factory. No one knows how it started. The floor was covered in paper and cloth scraps.

The fire spread quickly. It spread to the ninth floor. Cloth was everywhere—on the floor, on tables, and hanging from racks. It was a perfect place for a fire.

There were no fire extinguishers in the factory. All the workers had were 27 buckets of water, but that was not enough. They had a hose, but it did not work. It had holes in it.

A Stampede

Everyone panicked. Screams filled the rooms. The women and children tried to go out to the fire escape. But the door was locked.

They stampeded to the stairs. The door to the stairs pulled into the room. It was not one that pushed out. In their panic, they pushed against the door. They could not pull it open.

The flames spread and grew hotter. Wooden floors and tables caught on fire. People's clothes caught on fire. They could not get away.

Smoke filled the room. Everyone coughed and struggled to breathe. Many people broke the windows. Then they jumped out!

More than 60 people died as they jumped from the firetrap.

The fire department was slow to arrive. When they got there, the fire hoses could shoot water only to the seventh floor. The ladders reached only to the sixth and seventh floors.

Brave People Help

A brave elevator operator kept going back to the eighth floor. The elevator was built to hold 10 or 15 people. More than 30 crammed in.

Risking his life, the elevator operator returned again and again. He saved more than 100 people.

People in a tall building next door lowered ladders to the roof of the Triangle building. More than 100 people escaped this way.

But 146 people, including those who jumped, did not escape death.

New Laws

To prevent more disasters, the government passed new laws. Factory and office doors could not be locked. They had to open out, not in, so people could push them open. Floors had to be clean. Every room needed two exits and a fire extinguisher.

It was a hard way to learn a lesson. Today, workplaces are safer, and children do not work in factories in America.

Firefighters battle the flames at the Triangle Shirtwaist factory.

The Molasses Tank Rupture
DATAFILE

Timeline

September 1918

The Boston Red Sox win the World Series of
Baseball.

January 1919

A tank of molasses ruptures in Boston, killing 21.

Where is Boston, Massachusetts?

HERE

Key Terms

elevated train—a city train with tracks above the street

rupture—to burst open; to explode

tidal wave—a huge wave that travels a long way

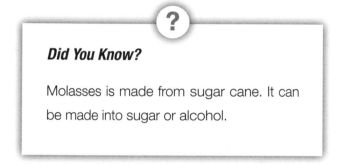

Did You Know?

Molasses is made from sugar cane. It can be made into sugar or alcohol.

The Molasses Tank Rupture

January 15, 1919, was a normal day in Boston. People went to work in elevated trains. Horses pulled wagons of goods. It was a calm, winter day.

Boston is a port, so ships were arriving and leaving filled with goods. One ship brought molasses from the Caribbean, where sugar cane grows.

The molasses was pumped into a huge tank. The tank was 50 feet tall and 90 feet across. It held 2.3 million gallons. The United States Industrial Alcohol Company planned to make the molasses into alcohol.

But the tank was not very strong, and it leaked. The company did not fix the leaks. Instead, they painted the tank brown so nobody could see the leaks. They did not solve the problem. They hid it.

Children knew about the leaks. After the tank was filled, they collected the molasses in cups and buckets. They ate some and took some home. The molasses tasted great on pancakes. Their mothers also cooked beans in molasses. They called it "Boston Baked Beans."

One warm day, something went wrong. Bolts started popping from the sides of the tank. Bam! Bam! Bam! They sounded like a machine gun.

A Tidal Wave

Suddenly, the tank ruptured. Pieces of steel went flying. A tidal wave of molasses rushed forward. The wave was 15 feet high—higher than some houses.

People could not believe what they were seeing. It seemed impossible. They did not know what it was.

Nothing could stop the wave. It was heavier than water. It moved in all directions at 35 miles per hour. It smashed and swallowed everything it hit.

Two children were collecting molasses when the tank ruptured. They disappeared under the giant wave.

Soon the wave picked up garbage, bricks, wood, barrels, horses, dogs, cats, rats, and other things. Some of the animals were still alive.

Drowned in Molasses

The wave hit houses, stores, wagons, cars, and boxcars. A firehouse collapsed under the wave. Many firemen were trapped under the rubble. One fireman named George Leahy drowned in the molasses.

The wave knocked over horses and their wagons. They were stuck to the pavement and covered with a heavy coat of molasses. They could not get up. They could not breathe.

Trapped in a Basement

Molasses rushed into a factory. The floor collapsed under the weight. Many workers fell into the basement.

The basement began to fill with the sticky, brown liquid. When the workers tried to run up the stairs, they slipped and fell. They were trapped as the molasses rose to their knees, their chests, their chins, and over their heads.

A Train Escapes

An elevated train came by. It passed just before the big, brown wave struck. The train escaped, but the track came down. The next train stopped just in time. People looked out the windows. They could not believe what they saw. The city was a sea of brown.

As houses and shops fell, people were trapped beneath them. No one could rescue them. It was impossible to walk in the sticky, brown streets.

Wagons got stuck in the stuff. Rescue equipment could not move. Everybody got trapped like bugs on flypaper.

Surfing Molasses

A boy named Anthony di Stasio was on his way home from school when the wave hit him. It carried him like a surfboard. Then it roared over him. He tumbled like a pebble in a stream.

Anthony was trapped under the river of molasses. It covered his face and filled his mouth. He choked and coughed. He could not breathe.

When rescue workers found him, they thought he was dead. They put him with the bodies of others who had died. Later, he woke up and saw his mother and sisters looking at him. They were surprised to see him open his eyes.

It took several days to find all the bodies. In all, 21 people were killed. Another 150 were injured. Many horses died.

A Very Sticky Mess

It was January, so the molasses was very thick and stiff. It was hard to walk in, hard to dig, and hard to move. It covered streets, walls, floors, cars, furniture—it covered everything!

When people walked in the molasses, they tracked it around the city. Little by little, the whole city got sticky.

Sidewalks were sticky. Wagon wheels were sticky. Train floors were sticky. House floors were sticky. Doorknobs and mailboxes were sticky. Chairs and beds were sticky. Mothers, fathers, children and pets were sticky. If it was in Boston, it was sticky.

Firemen sprayed salt water on the molasses. Slowly, little by little, the molasses washed away.

For years, Boston smelled like molasses. A brown line on buildings showed how deep it had been.

A Big Trial

Many people were mad about the disaster. The United States Industrial Alcohol Company said it was not their fault. They said somebody blew up the tank with dynamite.

A big trial was held in Boston. It started in August 1920 and took three years to sort through all the facts. People reported what they saw. They spoke about the leaks in the tank. They described how people died.

Experts said the tank was not strong enough. The court decided it was the company's fault. The company paid money to the victims' families. But that did not bring back lost loved ones.

New Laws

Nobody wanted to see another disaster like the molasses tank rupture. Massachusetts' government passed new laws. Tanks had to be extra strong—not just molasses tanks, but tanks for oil, water, and chemicals.

Big tanks are safer today. But some people say Boston still smells a little like molasses.

Do you know what "9-1-1" is?

9-1-1 is the phone number you call in any emergency. It is the same in every town. Anyone can call 9-1-1 in an emergency. If you see an accident or experience an emergency, dial 9-1-1.

How to call 9-1-1

It is easy to call 9-1-1. Just dial those numbers: 9 and 1 and 1. Wait until someone answers the phone. The person will ask you easy questions:

- What is your name? Where are you?
  What happened?

After you call 9-1-1

- Stay away from danger. Do not get trapped!
- When police or rescue workers arrive,
  tell them you called 9-1-1. Tell them
  what you saw.

Trapped Behind the Iron Curtain
DATAFILE

Timeline

August 1945
World War II ends.

August 1961
East Germany builds the Berlin Wall.

November 1989
People on both sides tear down the Berlin Wall.

Where is Germany?

HERE

Key Terms

hot air balloon—a huge balloon that carries passengers in a basket

Did You Know?

After World War II, Europe was divided into two parts by what Winston Churchill, in 1946, called the Iron Curtain. Britain, the United States, and their allies controlled the West. The Soviet Union controlled the East.

Trapped Behind the Iron Curtain

World War II ended in 1945. Two superpowers remained. On one side was the United States, France, and England. On the other side was the Soviet Union.

East and West Divided

The United States and the Soviet Union divided Europe into two areas: East and West. The West was free; the East was not.

Germany was split into two countries: East Germany and West Germany. Berlin, Germany's biggest city, was also split. It became East Berlin and West Berlin.

An Iron Curtain

There seemed to be an Iron Curtain between the East and the West. It was not an actual curtain. It was the border between the East and the West. Tanks and soldiers guarded the border. No one could cross it.

Trapped!

People in the East wanted to come to the West. They wanted freedom. They wanted a better life. But the Soviet government would not let them leave. They were trapped!

The problem was worse in Germany. The people of West Berlin were free to travel. But the people of East Berlin could not travel as easily.

Many East Germans fled to the West. The Soviet government did not like it. Their solution: build a long wall through the middle of Berlin. It was called the Berlin Wall.

The Berlin Wall

The Berlin Wall was huge. It was 96 miles long and 12 feet tall. It had barbed wire on top. Police dogs patrolled the wall. A trench ran along the wall. It was lit up at night. Guards in towers shot anyone who came too close.

The people of East Germany did not like being trapped. They did not like being separated from their families and friends on the other side. But if they complained, they were sent to prison.

In August 1961, people started escaping. They crashed through the wall with trucks. They hid in trains. They threw their babies over the wall to people in West Berlin.

But the wall did not cover canals and rivers, so people swam or sailed in boats to freedom. In winter, they walked across the thin ice.

The Berlin Wall

Tunnels to Freedom

Others dug tunnels under the wall. The tunnels started in basements and gardens in East Berlin. One tunnel started in a cemetery. People went to the cemetery with flowers. When no one was looking, they jumped into the tunnel and escaped.

A woman with a baby in a carriage found the cemetery tunnel. She took the baby and escaped. But she left the carriage behind. The police found it. Then they found the tunnel. They closed the tunnel before more people could escape.

Rope Against the Law

Many people climbed over the wall with ropes. To stop them, the government outlawed the sale of rope.

Then people made rope from string. More of them escaped. To stop them, the government outlawed the sale of string.

Balloons to Freedom

The Wetzel and Strelzyck families made a hot air balloon. They sewed together little patches of nylon cloth. Late one night, they opened the balloon in a field. Quickly they filled it with hot air. Slowly and quietly they sailed over the wall.

They were free!

Then government outlawed the sale of nylon cloth.

Someone else tried to fly over in a gas balloon. Sadly, it crashed before taking the pilot to freedom.

Shot While Escaping

From 1961 to 1989, more than 5,000 people tried to escape East Germany. Border police shot people trying to climb the wall. They shot a man trying to escape in a truck. They shot people swimming across a river. Others drowned in the river.

More than 100 people died as they tried to escape from the East.

The East Weakens

In 1989, The Soviet Union could no longer control East Germany or the other countries of the East.

On November 9, 1989, people on both sides attacked the wall. No one stopped them. They broke the wall with hammers and other tools. Piece by piece, they took it down.

The people of East Berlin flooded into the West. They were no longer trapped. There was a big celebration in Berlin.

The Iron Curtain Comes Down

On July 1, 1990, East Germany and West Germany were one country again, and they were free.

In December 1991, the Soviet Union divided into many countries. It was the end of the Soviet Union and the Iron Curtain.

Today, only a small part of the Berlin Wall remains. It is a reminder of the days of the Iron Curtain.

CHAPTER 4

The Kursk *Disaster*
DATAFILE

Timeline

January 1995

Russia launches a large submarine, the *Kursk*, for the first time.

August 2000

The *Kursk* sinks to the bottom of the Barents Sea.

Where is the Barents Sea?

HERE

Key Terms

air pocket—a small area of air underground or underwater

compartment—a room in a submarine

nuclear—relating to, or using atomic energy

nuclear reactor—an engine that creates power from fission—a chain reaction that splits atoms and releases their energy

torpedo compartment—a room where submarines store torpedoes

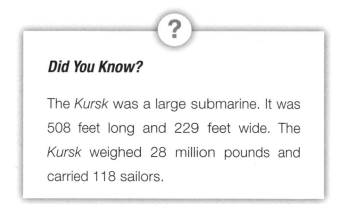

Did You Know?

The *Kursk* was a large submarine. It was 508 feet long and 229 feet wide. The *Kursk* weighed 28 million pounds and carried 118 sailors.

The Kursk *Disaster*

On August 12, 2000, a large Russian submarine cruised deep beneath the Barents Sea. It was the *Kursk*.

The waters were icy cold. The Barents Sea is in the Arctic Ocean.

The *Kursk* was a nuclear submarine. Nuclear reactors provide the forward and reverse thrust in the water. It could stay underwater for 100 days. It could go many miles without refueling.

Nobody knows exactly what happened on that terrible day. It is thought that without warning, the *Kursk*'s front torpedo compartment broke open. Tons of cold seawater flooded in. No one could stop it.

The Russian submarine *Kursk*.

Waterproof Doors

Submarines have strong doors between compartments. The doors are waterproof. Sailors open the doors only to walk through them. After they walk through a door, they close it.

If one of the compartments floods, the others will stay dry. The water will not fill the whole sub. The sub might sink, but some of the sailors might survive.

Pockets of Air

The *Kursk* sank more than 320 feet to the bottom of the Barents Sea. There were 118 sailors on board. Many men were killed when the torpedo compartment broke open. But some were still alive—trapped in pockets of air in the ninth compartment at the rear of the sub, far beneath the surface of the sea.

What caused the sub to flood? Maybe the *Kursk* hit another submarine. Maybe a torpedo exploded. Maybe the sub hit an old mine.

No Escape

The *Kursk* had three escape hatches. A rescue ship could lower an escape pod and attach it to the escape hatch. But the pod could only hold 10 sailors. It would take many trips to rescue all 118 men.

The torpedo compartment had an escape hatch. But the torpedo compartment was flooded. The sailors could not get to this escape hatch. There was another escape hatch near the control room. But it was damaged. It would not open. The control room in the center of the sub was also damaged by water.

A third escape hatch was at the rear of the sub. It was their only hope of escape. But the water of the Barents Sea was very cold. The surface was too far away for them to swim to safety. They were trapped. They could only wait to be rescued.

Ships to the Rescue

Russia quickly sent seven ships and three submarines to the rescue. On August 14, they found the *Kursk*. But it was hard to reach the sub. The weather was bad. The waves were more than 12 feet high.

On August 16, they lowered a rescue vehicle to the *Kursk*. It was difficult to work so deep under the sea. The water was murky. Rescuers could see only about six feet in front of them.

But they also had to work slowly and carefully. If the rescuers hit the sub, they might break it open. If they made a hole, the air might escape.

Running Out of Time

Some of the rescuers believed they could hear the crew banging on the sides of the submarine. But the crew must have been running out of air. They were running out of time!

There was no easy way to rescue the sailors. If the rescuers cut a hole in the sub, the air would escape. How would they get the sailors out of the sub and into the rescue vehicle?

Pulling the submarine up was impossible. It was 508 feet long, longer than a line of 12 school buses. It weighed more than 14,000 tons. Nothing could pull the *Kursk* up through more than 320 feet of water.

Time Ticks Away

At first, the United States, England, and Norway said they would help. The Russians said no. They thought they could do the job themselves.

Some experts said the sailors might have air for two more days. The Russians thought they might have air for another week.

Even a week was not enough time for a rescue. On Thursday, August 17, Russia asked for help.

LR5 Rescue Vehicle

Norway and England were the first to arrive. England had an underwater rescue vehicle. It was called an LR5. The LR5 was flown to Norway. Then a Norwegian ship took the LR5 to the scene.

The LR5 went down to the *Kursk*. Then divers swam up to the sub. The rescuers saw no signs of life. They did not hear any banging.

Divers saw a huge hole in the side of the *Kursk*. They thought maybe there had been two explosions.

They tried to open a hatch. They wanted to swim in and look around. They tried to open the front hatch. It would not move. It was damaged.

On Monday, August 21, divers opened the rear hatch. They swam into the sunken sub. It was completely flooded. They found no survivors.

All Hope Lost

The Russian government said there were no survivors. If anyone had been trapped alive, now they were dead.

That was the end of the rescue mission. Now the Russians had a new mission. They had to figure out what had gone wrong with the *Kursk*.

Russia Weeps

On August 22, Russian officials displayed the names of the *Kursk* crew on TV. It was a very sad time for Russia.

The sailors' families wanted to know why no one rescued the sailors in time. They were very sad and angry. They imagined what it had been like for their sons, fathers, and husbands who were trapped in the dark air pocket.

A Short Note

Divers continued to search the submarine. They wanted to know why it sank. They also wanted to know if anyone had been trapped alive.

They found a note on one of the sailors. It said that 23 of them had survived the explosion. After the front flooded, the survivors moved to the back. They tried to escape but could not get out. Because it was a short note, people think he did not live long.

Now What?

The Russians learned a lot from the *Kursk* disaster. They learned to ask for help when they needed it. If there is another submarine accident, then rescuing survivors might be easier.

Now all countries are more careful with their submarines. Nobody wants to be trapped under the sea.

The Quecreek Mine Flood
DATAFILE

Timeline

January 2001

George W. Bush becomes US president.

July 2002

The Quecreek Mine floods, trapping nine miners.

Where is Somerset, Pennsylvania?

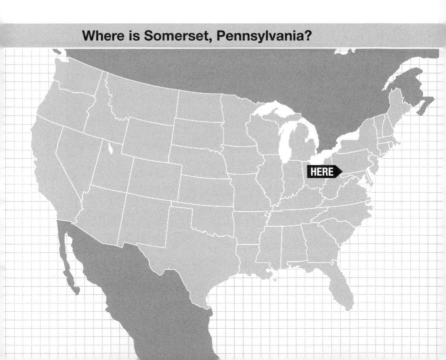

HERE

Key Terms

air pressure—the force of air in a closed space

drill bit—the part of a drill that cuts the hole

? Did You Know?

The deepest coal mine in America, the Blue Creek Mine, was 2,140 feet deep— almost half a mile underground. It was closed in 2001 after explosions killed 13 miners.

The Quecreek Mine Flood

The Quecreek coal mine was a new mine. Deep underground, it passed by the Saxon mine. The Saxon mine was closed in 1963 because it had flooded. Miners thought the Saxon mine was 300 feet away.

It Was Not That Far Away at All

On Wednesday, July 24, 2002, at about 8:50 pm., the miners drilled a hole in the wall. It broke through to the Saxon mine shaft. Water burst through the hole.

They did not know it yet, but there was 50 million gallons of icy cold water in the Saxon mine!

Get Out!

Water gushed into the Quecreek mine. A miner radioed to the workers.

"We hit water—get out!" — *Quecreek miner*

Most of the miners rushed toward the surface. But nine were on the other side of the flood. They had to go farther into the mountain to escape the flood. They scrambled to a high place in the mine.

The hole in the wall grew larger. Cold, dark water flooded in. The men who escaped waded through the cold water. They raced the flood half a mile to the surface.

Trapped!

The other nine men had no chance to escape. They were trapped! The water rose around them.

They were 240 feet beneath the surface of the earth and half a mile from the mine's entrance.

The men squeezed into a tiny pocket of air. The space was just three feet high and 12 feet long. The space was wet, cold, and dark.

Being trapped underground is a miner's worst fear. They thought rescue was almost impossible. All they could do was hope, pray, and shiver in the cold.

The men had wives and children. One had grandchildren. They did not want to die.

Rescue Teams

Above ground, hundreds of rescue workers did everything they could. To the rescue workers, this was not a job. They were saving their friends and coworkers.

First they drilled a small hole into the mine. They used maps of the mine to figure out where the men might be. They were hoping to hit an air pocket and find the trapped miners.

But finding that pocket of air was very hard. Imagine trying to dangle a 240-foot piece of string into a soda can in the dark. If you do not get it right the first time, nine people die. That is how hard it was.

The rescue began with a small hole. It was just six inches across. It had three purposes:

- The first purpose was to find out if the men were still alive.

- The second purpose was to give them air. If the men were alive, they needed fresh air.

- The third purpose was to increase the air pressure in the pocket of air. A higher air pressure would push the water away from the trapped men.

Frantically Working

At the same time, firemen pumped water out of the mine. Using 10 pumps, they moved more than 20,000 gallons per minute. At that rate, it would take almost 42 hours to pump the mine dry!

The drill bored through 240 feet of rock. The rescue workers did not drill fast. They drilled carefully. They had no time for mistakes.

Early Thursday morning, July 25th, the drill broke into the pocket of air. The men in the mine were very happy to see the drill bit. They were glad that their friends were trying to rescue them.

Alive!

At about midday on Thursday, the workers put a long pipe down the hole. The men in the mine banged on the pipe. The rescue workers heard it. They knew the trapped men were alive!

Above ground, everyone cheered. There was still hope. But there was still a lot of work to do, too. The men were very cold and hungry. They did not have much time.

That first hole was just a start. Men could not fit through a six-inch pipe. They needed a larger hole.

On Thursday night, they started to drill a second hole beside the first one. It was three feet wide— wide enough for a man to pass through.

Inch by Inch

The larger drill was slower. Inch by inch, it worked through the rock. They drilled all night and all the next day. As they drilled, they lowered the pipe further down into the hole.

The whole town watched. In fact, TV crews reported the event. People across the country watched the drama.

A little after midnight on Friday morning, the drill snapped! The drill bit was stuck in the rock 110 feet down.

Helicopter to the Rescue

It took 18 hours to free the broken drill bit. A helicopter brought another bit to the scene.

Late Friday night, they started drilling again. Down below, the men were suffering. The wet chill was enough to kill them. They hugged each other to stay warm.

Then, water rose to the first drill hole. The men had to move away from it.

Last Meal

One of the men had half a sandwich. He shared it with the others. It was their only food for the past three days. They thought it might be their last meal.

The rescue workers were suffering, too. They had no time to sleep, no time to eat. They worked all day and all night.

At 3:30 p.m. on Saturday July 27, the drill pipe broke. Everyone waited until new pipe came in by helicopter.

Drilling continued, inch-by-inch.

At 10:35 p.m. on Saturday, the drill broke into the air pocket. Workers lowered a phone to the trapped miners. The miners said everyone was alive.

But they needed help. One man had chest pains. They all needed food and heat. The cold was killing them.

Nine helicopters waited to take the men to a hospital. There was still work to do. Workers removed the drill. They lowered a rescue basket down the pipe.

The basket was like a cage. It was just 22 inches wide. The basket carried food and drink for the men. After eating, the first man climbed into the basket.

On Sunday, July 28, at 1:00 a.m., rescuers lifted Randy Fogle to the surface. He was the first miner saved. At 2:45 a.m., Mark Popernack came into the spotlights and fresh air. He was the last miner saved.

Cheers and Tears

Everyone cheered. Many cried. The men were wrapped in blankets. After doctors checked each one, he was taken to a hospital.

"What a beautiful ending! We're nine for nine, and we got all our guys out."
— Mark Schweiker, Governor of Pennsylvania

Lessons Learned

Miners learned many things from the Quecreek accident. They learned that they cannot always trust underground maps. They also learned not to give up hope.

Upper Big Branch Mine
DATAFILE

Timeline

December 6, 1907

A methane explosion ignites coal dust in the Monongah Mine. The exact death toll is unknown, but it is estimated that more than five hundred miners died as a result of the explosions.

April 5, 2010

Undetected high levels of methane cause an explosion in West Virginia's Upper Big Branch mine, killing twenty-nine workers.

Where is West Virginia?

HERE

Key Terms

calibrate—to check an instrument for accuracy and to make adjustments if necessary

methane—a colorless, odorless flammable gas that is the main component of natural gas

railway tie—a wood or concrete rectangle used as a base for railroad tracks

restitution—to compensate for damage or loss

retirement—leaving your job or career for good. Usually around the mid-60 years of age

?

Did You Know?

Coal is a fossil fuel. It looks like shiny black rock. When coal is burned, it makes heat. It was originally used t0 heat homes in the 1800s.We burn coal today to make electricity.

CHAPTER 6

Upper Big Branch Mine

"If I die tomorrow," said Benny Ray Willingham, "I've lived a good life."

Willingham, 61, was just a few short weeks away from retiring. He worked as a coal miner at the Upper Big Branch Mine in Montcoal, West Virginia. Montcoal is about 30 miles south of Charleston. The mine was owned by Massey Energy.

Willingham and his wife Edie Mae were planning a trip. They wanted to go to the Virgin Islands to celebrate his retirement. Spending time with their three kids and six grandkids was also part of the plan.

But it was not to be.

On April 5, 2010, the Upper Big Branch Mine exploded.

At 3:02 in the afternoon there was a huge blast. Benny Ray Willingham and 28 other miners were killed. Two others were injured.

Rescue workers said the blast site was like nothing they'd ever seen. Big machines were blown to bits. Railway ties were twisted like pretzels.

The rescue search went on for several days. Four workers were unaccounted for. It turned out they had died in the blast. The twisted wreckage made it nearly impossible to find their bodies.

Timothy Davis Sr., 51, was among the dead. He was known as "Big Tim." Big Tim had been married to his wife Diana for 30 years. Two of his nephews, Josh Napper and Cory Davis, were also killed in the blast. His brother Tommy made it out alive. So did his nephew Cody.

In 2000, Big Tim was injured in an earlier mining accident. A boulder fell on him, smashing his face. He lost all his teeth and had to have his face put back together surgically. But he returned to the mines. He did it to provide for his family.

Big Tim's nephew Josh was 25 when he was killed. He had been working in the mines for only two months. Known for lifting weights, Josh could bench-press 500 pounds. He had a baby daughter who was only 20 months old.

Men of all ages worked in the Upper Big Branch Mine. Most were family men. Many of those who died came from mining families. Their family members had worked in the mines for generations.

There are few women miners—only about 2 percent. All the workers killed in the Upper Big Branch Mine explosion were men.

People all over the world depend on coal. More than 40 percent of the electricity in the US is produced with coal. Without coal, we'd have much less power for our lights, televisions, and computers.

Coal miners have a hard life. Every day they go underground into the mines. They come up at the end of their shift covered in black coal dust. It's dirty, dangerous work. They know they might not come back up.

But they can't beat the pay. Young people right out of high school can make $50,000 a year or more. In rural West Virginia, that's good money. It's enough to own a home and raise a family. West Virginia has more coal miners than any other state.

The Upper Big Branch Mine explosion was the worst in 40 years. In 1970, a mine disaster in Kentucky killed 38 men. The worst mine disaster ever was in 1907. The Monongah Nos. 6 and 8 mines exploded in Illinois, killing an estimated 500 men and boys. Since then, laws have changed to protect workers.

A section on the Upper Big Branch Mine on April 6, 2010, in Montcoal, West Virginia.

Sad to say, sometimes companies put profits before people. Massey Energy cut corners to make more money. They broke laws that ended up causing 29 people to die.

After the explosion, West Virginia's governor ordered an investigation. The investigative report said the accident was the fault of Massey Energy. It said the Mine Safety and Health Administration (MSHA) was also at fault. They did not enforce the laws like they were supposed to.

The report said Massey Energy had operated in a "profoundly reckless manner." It said the 29 miners would not have died if Massey had complied with mining regulations.

The explosion was caused by methane gas and coal dust. The equipment to measure the gas needed to be calibrated every 30 days. But it had not been checked for over three months. The owners did not want to shut down the mine for a few hours to calibrate the equipment.

Massey Energy was sold to Alpha Natural Resources. In December 2011, Alpha settled a lawsuit about the Upper Big Branch explosion. They paid $210 million in fines to avoid prosecution and to provide restitution, or make amends for wrongdoing.

Even though Massey was sold, its executives are still responsible. Federal prosecutors filed charges against several mine executives, including one mine supervisor.

Two Stephanies
DATAFILE

Timeline

August 16, 2008

Stephanie Nielson and her husband are flying from Arizona to New Mexico when the small plane they are in crashes mid-flight.

March 2, 2012

Marysville, Indiana, resident Stephanie Decker is at home with two of her children when a deadly tornado reduces their three-story home to rubble.

Where is Indiana?

HERE

Key Terms

blogger—a person who keeps and updates a blog (a website where people record opinions, information, etc. on a regular basis)

coma—a state of deep unconsciousness that lasts for a prolonged or indefinite period

debris—scattered fragments, typically of something wrecked or destroyed

prosthetics—artificial body parts

resolve—firm determination to do something

?

Did You Know?

The rule of nines allows doctors to assess the severity of a burn victim's injuries. The body is divided into nine sections with a percentage assigned to each section.

Two Stephanies

Stephanie Decker

Motherhood is a powerful thing. Hunters know not to mess with a mother grizzly. She will do anything to protect her cubs.

This is the story of two human moms who would do anything for their kids. Both are named Stephanie. And both moms are heroines.

Stephanie Decker lives in Marysville, Indiana. She lost both legs while protecting her kids from a tornado.

On March 2, 2012, a swarm of 130 tornadoes hit several states. A total of 40 people were killed in the deadly storms. Today, Stephanie considers herself lucky.

"Losing my legs meant nothing in comparison to what I still had," she told ABC News. Her kids and her husband were unharmed. Their house, however, was completely destroyed.

Stephanie was home with her two youngest kids when the monster tornado hit. She rushed Dominic, 8, and Reese, 6, to the basement. But windows started popping throughout the house. The loud winds roared all around.

Stephanie felt her children would be sucked up into the tornado or hurt by flying debris. So she grabbed a comforter. She wrapped it around both kids. Then she lay on top of them.

Just as she did, a huge beam fell on her legs. The pain was horrific. Stephanie said it felt like a blowtorch on her legs. She knew it was bad. She would bleed to death if she didn't get help soon.

Dominic ran for help. Soon Stephanie was in the hospital.

The aftermath of an ER-4 tornado that touched down in Henryville, Indiana, on March 2, 2012, about 10 miles from Marysville.

Doctors said it would be at least a year before she walked again. But she proved them wrong. On May 24, 2012, she appeared on the *Ellen De-Generes Show.* The crowd roared its approval as Stephanie stood up and walked. This was only two months after she lost both legs.

Stephanie was wearing new prosthetics. The plastic and metal parts replaced her missing lower legs and feet. She joked about not needing to paint her toenails anymore.

During her recovery, Stephanie had a goal. She wanted to walk out on the stage on *Ellen.* The whole Decker family had looked forward to being on the show. The warm-hearted talk-show host was one of their favorites.

Stephanie's dream came true when she appeared on Ellen. She rolled out onto the stage in a power wheelchair.

A walker was brought out for her. Using a lever, she hoisted herself up from the wheelchair. She placed the prosthetics inside the walker. As she stood up and walked, the crowd clapped wildly and cheered her on.

Stephanie Nielson

Another heroic mom named Stephanie was in a fiery plane crash.

It was around 3:45 p.m. on August 16, 2008. Stephanie Nielson and her husband, Christian, lived in Arizona. They were flying in a small plane to New Mexico.

Christian was flying the plane. He had just gotten his pilot's license. His flight instructor flew with them. They were returning home after spending the day in New Mexico. Their four kids stayed in Mesa, Arizona, with their grandma.

This Cessna small airplane is similar to the Cessna 177 Cardinal that was piloted by flight instructor Doug Kinneard when it crashed at takeoff in St. Johns, Arizona.

A little while later the plane's motor died. The small plane dropped out of the sky. It crashed onto a woodpile. Gallons of jet fuel spilled out onto the wood and caught fire.

A man held Stephanie as they waited for the ambulance.

"What are my babies going to think of me?" she asked him. "Please don't let me die."

Stephanie and Christian were badly burned. Stephanie was burned over 80 percent of her body.

Doctors used medication to keep her in a coma for three months. It was so they could heal her burns. It required many surgeries. Stephanie will continue to need surgeries for the rest of her life.

When she woke up from the coma, Stephanie felt she had a choice. She could go to heaven. Or she could stay and face a lot of pain because of her burns. But by hanging on to life, she would be able to help her family.

She resolved to stay and raise her kids. Her strong will to live carried her through the pain.

When she went home, her face was badly scarred. At first her children were afraid of her. She didn't look like their mom. But with her love and care they soon got used to her again.

Stephanie Nielson now lives in Utah. She is a well-known mommy blogger. Her blog is called the NieNie Dialogues. To her thousands of readers, Stephanie is Supermom. She writes about the joys of motherhood.

Many of her readers are not mothers. They simply like reading Stephanie's uplifting stories.

On April 3, 2012, Stephanie gave birth to her fifth child, Charlotte.

Chilean Miners
DATAFILE

Timeline

June 19, 1945

A fire breaks out in Chile's El Teniente copper mine; 355 trapped men die of smoke inhalation.

January 20, 2006

An explosion in the Carola-Agustina copper mine in Copiapo, Chile, kills two and traps 70 miners.

August 5, 2010

The San José copper mine in Copiapo, Chile, collapses, trapping 33 men underground.

Where is Chile?

HERE

Key Terms

morale—the confidence, enthusiasm, and discipline of a person or group at a particular time

ration—a fixed amount of food or water allowed to each person during a time of shortage

smoke inhalation—breathing in the harmful gases, vapors, and particulate matter contained in smoke

ventilation shaft—a shaft or duct, which serves as an air passage for ventilation

?

Did You Know?

Mining is one of the world's most dangerous occupations. China is the deadliest country for miners. A Chinese miner is 100 times more likely to die in a mining accident than a US miner.

Chilean Miners

The tiny note was scribbled in red marker. It said: "*Estamos bien en el refugio, los 33.*" The English translation was this: "We are well in the shelter, the 33." The 33 miners were trapped in a mine 2,300 feet under the ground near Copiapo, Chile.

Seventeen days earlier, on August 5, 2010, the San Jose copper mine had collapsed. Trapped under the surface were 32 Chileans and one Bolivian. They ranged in age from 19 to 63.

After the cave-in, the men realized they were trapped. They were very organized. They knew they had to keep their spirits up to survive.

At first the men tried to get out through the ventilation shafts. But there were no ladders. The mining company had been ordered to install ladders. But they failed to do so. The owners wanted to save money.

The mine was 120 years old. It had a lot of safety issues. For that reason, the men in the San Jose mine made more money than men working in safer mines.

They had to carefully ration their food supplies, too. The food they had was only meant to last two or three days. But by being very careful, the men made it last two weeks. Their leader was a man named Luis Urzua, age 54. His calmness and sense of humor were credited with helping keep all the men alive.

Most of the men were Catholic. Their strong religious faith helped them survive. Mario Gomez and Jose Henriquez were their religious leaders. They helped keep up morale by leading prayers.

Up on the surface, a $20 million rescue operation was underway. Engineers bored several six-inch-wide holes looking for the men. Each shaft reached a dead end. People were starting to lose hope that the men were still alive.

Finally, after 17 days, the engineers drilled a hole in the right place. They found the men. The red-lettered note told them the men were still alive. Once the rescuers knew that, they swung into high gear. Help poured in from everywhere.

People all over the world embraced the red-lettered message. Soon it appeared on websites, banners, and T-shirts. The words, "*Estamos bien en el refugio, los 33,"* became the motto for the remaining 53 days of the rescue operation. People all over the world followed the rescue events by TV and Internet.

The rescuers started sending capsules down the hole. These containers held medical supplies, blankets, notes from their families, and most importantly, food. The miners had run out of food shortly before they were found. After that the miners were sent food from the surface every day.

Four days after the miners were located, video cameras were sent down. The men videotaped each other. The videos were broadcast all over the world.

In the first voice recording sent to the surface, Urzua didn't let on about how scared the men were. He just said, "We're fine, waiting for you to rescue us."

Urzua organized the miners in their underground shelter. The men had a one-man, one-vote system for making decisions. They worked together to keep up morale. And they did all they could to try to escape. To help the rescuers find them, Urzua made maps of where they were.

Over two months later, on October 13, they emerged.

When the miners finally came into view, perhaps a billion people were watching. Some viewed it on TV as the miners came out into the fresh air. Others saw it on the Internet. People cheered or wept with joy. Everyone was relieved that the miners finally made it out.

After the rescue, the men were given sunglasses to protect their eyes from bright light. They were tired, but they were in good spirits and relatively healthy.

Some of the men had developed dental and eye problems. Two men developed *silicosis,* a serious lung disease. Others had psychological problems. But otherwise they were okay.

After their ordeal, the men were treated like superstars. They were given trips to Greece and Disneyland. Each of *"Los 33"* was given a free Kawasaki motorcycle.

But a year later, many of them were not doing so well. Some still had medical problems. Others suffered from a psychological problem called *post-traumatic stress disorder.* This causes nightmares, sleeping problems, and other issues.

Some, however, experienced post-traumatic *growth.* The experience made them stronger. Mario Sepulveda is one of these. With his outgoing nature, Sepulveda was the spokesman in the video recordings of the trapped men. He went on to make a career out of speaking about the ordeal.

In July 2011, Hollywood producer Mike Medavoy bought the rights to make a movie about the trapped miners. Filming is scheduled to begin in 2012. The miners will make money from the movie based on the story of their ordeal.

Glossary

air pocket—a small area of air underground or underwater

air pressure—the force of air in a closed space

blogger—a person who keeps and updates a blog (website on which an individual or group of users record opinions, information, etc. on a regular basis)

calibrate—to check an instrument for accuracy and to make adjustments if necessary

coma—a state of deep unconsciousness that lasts for a prolonged or indefinite period

compartment—a room in a submarine

debris—scattered fragments, typically of something wrecked or destroyed

drill bit—the part of a drill that cuts the hole

elevated train—a city train with tracks above the street

fire escape—stairs outside a building that give people a way to escape a fire

hot air balloon—a huge balloon that carries passengers in a basket

inspector—a person who is hired to check for problems

methane—a colorless, odorless flammable gas that is the main component of natural gas

morale—the confidence, enthusiasm, and discipline of a person or group at a particular time

nuclear—relating to, or using atomic energy

nuclear reactor—an engine that creates power from fission—a chain reaction that splits atoms and releases their energy

prosthetics—artificial body parts

railway tie—a wood or concrete rectangle used as a base for railroad tracks

ration—a fixed amount of food or water allowed to each person during a time of shortage

resolve—firm determination to do something

restitution—to compensate for damage or loss

retirement—leaving your job or career for good. Usually around the mid-60 years of age.

rupture—to burst open; to explode

smoke inhalation—breathing in the harmful gases, vapors, and particulate matter contained in smoke

sweatshop—a hot, crowded, unsafe shop or factory in which employees work long hours at low wages

tidal wave—a huge wave that travels a long way

torpedo compartment—a room where submarines store torpedoes

ventilation shaft—a shaft or duct, which serves as an air passage for ventilation

Index